The Methuen
Audition Book for Women

Annika Bluhm is herself an actress and
worked for one year at French's Bookshop,
prior to training at the Guildhall School of
Music and Drama. In the course of
compiling this collection of fifty audition
speeches from some of our finest
contemporary playwrights, she
interviewed a number of directors from
small companies to major institutions. She
has also compiled and edited The Methuen
Audition Book for Men.

The Methuen Audition Book for Women

Compiled by
ANNIKA BLUHM

Methuen Drama

First published in Great Britain by Methuen Drama Ltd
Michelin House, 81 Fulham Road, London SW3 6RB
and distributed in the United States of America
by HEB Inc, 70 Court Street, Portsmouth, New Hampshire 03801.

A CIP catalogue record for this book is available
from the British Library.

ISBN 0 413 61300 3

Typeset by Hewer Text Composition Services, Edinburgh
Printed and bound in Great Britain by Cox & Wyman Ltd, Reading

ACKNOWLEDGEMENTS

Grateful acknowledgement is made for permission to reprint extracts from copyrighted material:

Accrington Pals by Peter Whelan; copyright© 1984, Methuen Drama. **Adult Child/Dead Child** by Claire Dowie; published in *Plays by Women VII* (ed. Mary Remnant); copyright© 1988, Methuen Drama. **And A Nightingale Sang . . .** by C. P. Taylor; copyright© 1987, Methuen Drama. **The Art Of Success** by Nick Dear; copyright© 1988, Methuen Drama. **Bazaar And Rummage** by Sue Townsend; copyright © 1987, Methuen Drama. **The Castle** by Howard Barker; copyright© 1985, John Calder (Publishers) Ltd, 18 Brewer Street, London W1R 4AS. **Chameleon** by Michael Ellis; published in *Black Plays I* (ed. Yvonne Brewster); copyright© 1987, Methuen Drama. **City Sugar** by Stephen Poliakoff; copyright© 1978, Methuen Drama. **Confusions** by Alan Ayckbourn; copyright© 1987, Methuen Drama. **Donkey's Years** by Michael Frayn; published in *Frayn: Plays One*; copyright© 1985, Methuen Drama. **Educating Rita** by Willy Russell; copyright© 1985, Methuen Drama. **Fear And Misery In The Third Reich** by Bertolt Brecht; copyright© 1979, Suhrkamp Verlag, Frankfurt am Main. **Fen** by Caryl Churchill; copyright© 1983, Methuen Drama. **Find Me** by Olwen Wymark; copyright© 1983, Methuen Drama. **Fugue** by Rona Munro; Copyright© Margaret Ramsay Ltd, 14a Goodwin's Court, London WC2N 4LL. **Great Celestial Cow** by Sue Townsend; copyright© 1984, Methuen Drama. **Joyriders** by Christina Reid; copyright© 1987, Methuen Drama. **Letters Home** by Rose Leiman Goldenberg published in plays by Women II (ed. Mary Remnant); copyright© 1983, Methuen Drama. **Made In Bangkok** by Anthony Minghella; copyright© 1988, Methuen Drama. **Made In Spain** by Tony Grounds; published in the *1986 Verity Bargate Award Plays* (ed. Barrie Keeffe); copyright© 1986, Methuen Drama. **Making Noise Quietly** by Robert Holman; copyright© 1987, Methuen Drama. **Map Of The World** by David Hare; copyright© 1983, Faber and Faber Ltd, 3 Queens Square, London WC1N 3AU. **Messiah** by Martin Sherman; copyright© 1982, Amber Lane Press Ltd, Church Street, Charlbury, Oxon OX7 3PR. **My Mother Said I Never Should** by Charlotte Keatley; copyright© 1988, Methuen Drama. **The Normal Heart** by Larry Kramer; copyright© 1987, Methuen Drama and Margaret Ramsay Ltd, 14a Goodwin's Court, St. Martin's Lane, London WC2N 4LL. **Not With A Bang** by Mike Harding; copyright © 1984, Mike Harding. Reprinted by permission of the author's agent: Margaret Ramsay Ltd, 14a Goodwin's Court, St Martin's Lane, London WC2 4LL. **Our Country's Good** by Timberlake Wertenbaker; copyright© 1988, Methuen Drama. **Ourselves Alone** by Anne Devlin; copyright© 1986, Faber and Faber Ltd, 3 Queen Square, London WC1N 3AU. **Plenty** by David Hare; copyright© 1978, Faber and Faber Ltd, 3 Queen Square, London WC1N 3AU and New American Library, 1663 Broadway, New York, NY 10019, USA. **Raspberry** by Tony Marchant; copyright© 1983, Methuen Drama. **Road** by Jim Cartwright; copyright© 1986, Methuen Drama. **Rose** by Andrew Davies; copyright© 1980, Andrew Davies. Reprinted by permission of the author's agent: Harvey, Unna & Stephen Durbridge Ltd, 24 Pottery Lane, Holland Park, London W11 4LZ. **Serious Money** by Caryl Churchill; copyright© 1987, Methuen Drama. **Shirley Valentine** by Willy Russell; copyright© 1988, Methuen Drama. **Spell #7** by Ntozake Shange; copyright© 1986, Methuen Drama and A. M. Heath & Co. Ltd, 79 St. Martin's Lane, London WC2N 4AA. **Stars** by Stephen Lowe; copyright© 1985, Methuen Drama. **Summer** by Edward Bond; copyright© 1987, Methuen Drama. **Teendreams** by David Edgar and Susan Todd; copyright © 1979, Methuen Drama. **Thatcher's Women** by Kay Adshead; published in *Plays by Women VII* (ed. Mary Remnant); copyright© 1988, Methuen Drama. **Touched** by Stephen Lowe; copyright© 1979, Methuen Drama. **True, Dare, Kiss** by Debbie Horsfield; published in *The Red Devil's Trilogy*; copyright© 1986, Methuen Drama. **Up To You, Porky** by Victoria Wood; copyright© 1986, Methuen Drama. **Waking Up** by Dario Fo and Franca Rame; published in *One Woman Plays*; copyright© 1981, Methuen Drama. **Whale Music** by Anthony Minghella; copyright© 1987, Samuel French, 52 Fitzroy Street, London W1P 6JR. **When I Was A Girl I Used To Scream And Shout** by Sharman MacDonald; copyright© 1985, Faber and Faber Ltd, 3 Queen Square, London WC1N 3AU.

Contents

Author's Acknowledgements

I would like to thank the following people for all their help, encouragement and advice during the compilation of this book: Lucy Alexander, Annie Castledine, Rachel Cooke, Lindsey Coulson, John Cullen, Richard Eyre, Vanessa Fielding, Powell Jones, Teresa McElroy, Johnathan Petherbridge, Virginia Snyders and Erika Spotswoode.

My special thanks to Jonathan Dow and Emma Rice who had to put up with more tantrums, sulks and general bad behaviour than anyone should have to and wearily accepted my opening gambit of 'What do you think of this speech . . . ?' every time.

And thank you to Pamela Edwardes, Peggy Butcher and Linda Brandon who bemusedly watched me bounce around the Methuen office for the entire summer and only occasionally asked me gently if I was actually working.

This book is the result of a Christmas conversation in Toronto and is therefore for my parents who believe anything is possible.

Annika Bluhm
Derby
1989